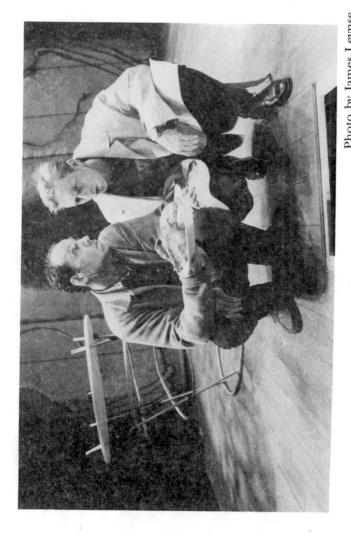

Photo by James Leynse

A scene from the Primary Stages production of "Missing/Kissing" Set design by Brad Stokes.

MISSING/
KISSING

MISSING MARISA
KISSING CHRISTINE

BY JOHN PATRICK SHANLEY

★

DRAMATISTS
PLAY SERVICE
INC.

MISSING/KISSING was produced by Primary Stages (Casey Childs, Artistic Director; Seth Gordon, Associate Producer) in New York City, on October 2, 1996. It was directed by John Patrick Shanley; the set design was by Brad Stokes; the costume design was by Laura Cunningham; the lighting design was by Brian Nason; the original music and sound design were by David Van Tieghem; and the stage manager was Bridget Murray Edwards. The cast was as follows:

MISSING MARISA
ELI ....Daniel Oreskes
TERRY ....Jake Weber

KISSING CHRISTINE
CHRISTINE .... Laura Hughes
LARRY..Jake Weber
SERVER.. Reiko Aylesworth

MISSING/KISSING received a world premiere under the title STRANGE ENCOUNTERS, in the 1996 Humana Festival of New America Plays at Actors Theatre of Louisville, (Jon Jory, Artistic Director) in Louisville, Kentucky, in March, 1996. It was directed by Douglas Hughes; the set design was by Paul Owen; the costume design was by Jeanette deJong; the lighting design was by T. J. Gerckens; the sound design was by Michael Rasbury; the dramaturg was Val Smith; and the stage manager was Janette L. Hubert. The cast was as follows:

MISSING MARISA
ELI ....Daniel Oreskes
TERRY .... Christopher Evan Welch

KISSING CHRISTINE
CHRISTINE .... Laura Hughes
LARRY.. Christopher Evan Welch
SERVER ....Elaine C. Bell

TABLE OF CONTENTS

MISSING MARISA

PROLOGUE

The actress who will play the Server in Kissing Christine *comes out and addresses the audience.*

ACTRESS.   We thought we'd start this double bill off with a poem. Music please. (*Music plays. In the spirit of a music box. She dances a poetic little dance. And then draws a finger across her throat. The music stops abruptly. She recites the poem.*)

> I water my plant
> When my plant is dry
> If I watered it wet
> My plant would die
>
> Don't kiss between kisses
> And weaken the kiss
> Most kisses are misses
> Connection is bliss

That's the poem. (*She curtsies and exits. The lights go down.*)

MISSING MARISA

When the lights come up, we discover two men, Terry and Eli.

Terry sits at a coffee counter on a high stool in Eli's kitchen. He has a cup of coffee. He's about 35. He's flushed with drink, though he's not at all drunk. He's handsome and maybe a little dissipated. His hand shakes a little. His clothes are fancy and casual and he wears them well.

Eli is sitting lower and slightly more down front, at a card table in a folding metal chair. He also has a cup of coffee. He's a little older or younger than Terry. He wears a somewhat rumpled businessman's shirt and trousers.

It is end of day. Some daylight, some twilight.

Both of these guys are tired.

ELI. Cake?

TERRY. No. No cake.

ELI. It's good to see you, Terry.

TERRY. It's good to see you, Eli.

ELI. How's the coffee?

TERRY. Black.

ELI. How's Marisa?

TERRY. I stopped seeing her. She stopped seeing me. She's gone. I don't know where she is. I just bought some land.

ELI. Where?

TERRY. Up in the Hudson River Valley.

ELI. The Mesopotamia of New York State!

TERRY. Yes. Thirteen acres.

ELI. Thirteen! The number of guests at the Last Supper!

TERRY. Well actually, it's 12.84 acres.

ELI. Good. That destroys the negative significance.

TERRY. There's a stream down the middle of the property. Hemlock trees.

ELI. Hemlock!

TERRY. That's what the realty guy told me, but don't take it to heart.

ELI. Don't take it internally, that's the point.

TERRY. I planted tulip bulbs I bought at a state fair I fell into while wandering upstate, looking for a life that makes sense to me.

ELI. Are you alright?

TERRY. WHAT DOES THAT MEAN?! *(Silence.)* I'm grateful you could meet me for coffee, have me for coffee, have coffee with me.

ELI. It's fun for me, too.

TERRY. Any kind of contact is hard now.

ELI. You mean, for you?

TERRY. No. I mean any kind of contact is hard now. Do you think I'm wrong?

ELI.   No.

TERRY.   The coffee's enjoyable. It's good. It's serviceable. It's the better for me being able to tell somebody it's good. And it's almost gone.

ELI.   I feel like the depth of your.... You're speaking from a different head than I'm at.

TERRY.   Can you get this head?

ELI.   No. I have my own head.

TERRY.   This coffee's unusual. This coffee's weak *at the bottom.*

ELI.   Should we speak of something obvious? Obviously, we have something new in common.

TERRY.   What?

ELI.   Marisa.

TERRY.   We already had Marisa in common.

ELI.   Yeah, but now we have her more deeply in common. For now, not only have we both loved her, now we've both lost her. Lost her irrevocably.

TERRY.   I took her away from you.

ELI.   Understandably, Terry, that's how you've always seen it. But you didn't take Marisa away from me.

TERRY.   Then what happened?

ELI.   Did she leave you for somebody else?

TERRY.   No.

ELI.   Is she with someone else?

TERRY.   No. I don't know. I don't think so. It's unlikely.

ELI.   Why?

TERRY.   It's highly unlikely.

ELI.   Why?

TERRY.   Because she has the clap. *(Pause.)*

ELI.   She has the clap?

TERRY.   Yes.

ELI.   Do you have the clap?

TERRY.   Yes.

ELI.   You do?

TERRY.   Yes, I've got it alright.

ELI.   So she got it from you?

TERRY.   No, she gave it to me.

ELI.   You're sure?

TERRY. Yes.

ELI. Where'd she get it?

TERRY. Well, that's where it gets tricky.

ELI. She won't say?

TERRY. Oh, she'll say, but what she says is, she says it's not the clap. But there on the other hand is my doctor. And my doctor would beg to differ. My doctor says it is most definitely the clap. He says me and her, we're applause. You haven't got the clap, have you?

ELI. No.

TERRY. I'm hungry.

ELI. Do you want me to get you something?

TERRY. That'd be very kind of you.

ELI. What do you want?

TERRY. If I knew that I wouldn't be SO FUCKING HUNGRY!

ELI. Marisa didn't jump off you for somebody?

TERRY. Not to my knowledge.

ELI. And you didn't give her the clap?

TERRY. She gave it to me!

ELI. Then where'd she get if from?

TERRY. She says she doesn't have it.

ELI. But she does.

TERRY. How the fuck do you know?

ELI. Because you told me.

TERRY. She's got it.

ELI. Then who gave it to her and how do you know she didn't go to that guy?

TERRY. Outta what, gratitude?

ELI. Outta just, you know, the inevitable.

TERRY. Everything's outta the inevitable.

ELI. Alright, alright, have your caveats. *(Pause.)*

TERRY. My goal is to be empty and say a prayer that something comes. But every time emptiness draws nigh, I get clawed open by this like Bengal tiger hunger and I end up ... begging.

ELI. Begging what?

TERRY. At the foot of some stone Madonna. The desperate man shuns the quiet, Eli. Shuns the quiet like Dracula shunned

12

the sun. Life was death to him. Life is death to me. That's the hunger that sucks my own blood and makes me weak and weaker as I feed.

ELI.   She left us both. I've been offered a job.

TERRY.   So what?

ELI.   Well that's a big area arena of life.

TERRY.   Not to me.

ELI.   Hmm.

TERRY.   Are you gonna take it?

ELI.   Don't you want to know what it is?

TERRY.   A job is what you make it.

ELI.   Don't you want to know what I'd make it?

TERRY.   No.

ELI.   Jump back! Do you have any interest in me?

TERRY.   I don't know.

ELI.   Can you really see me? Do you even know I'm here?

TERRY.   Alright, what's the job?

ELI.   A teacher for musically gifted people who've been overlooked by the school system of Southern New England.

TERRY.   That job, that job'd be totally quality dependent on the performance of the recruitment person who finds the students who you would subsequently teach.

ELI.   That's true.

TERRY.   Is that job open?

ELI.   The recruitment person job?

TERRY.   Yeah.

ELI.   Are you looking for a job?

TERRY.   I am noticing opportunities. If you got me a job, if you *wanted* to get me a job, I would know that you were inherent in, to, Marisa leaving me.

ELI.   Do you have any experience in the musical area?

TERRY.   It would be guilt help.

ELI.   I mean, I've been to your apartment, Terry. You don't have a piano.

TERRY.   The goodness of Judas.

ELI.   I'm sure Mr. Iscariot had his points.

TERRY.   I would know that you gave Marisa the clap. So I would know that you gave me the clap. Did you give me the clap?

ELI. No.

TERRY. Have you got the clap?

ELI. No.

TERRY. Have you recently been cured of the clap?

ELI. No. *(Pause.)* Not recently. But you say Marisa says she doesn't have the clap?

TERRY. But she gave it to me!

ELI. You're sure you've got it?

TERRY. I've been diagnosed! I'm under treatment.

ELI. For the clap?

TERRY. For the clap. Not recently. So you've had the clap?

ELI. In my life.

TERRY. Really?

ELI. Uh-huh. *(The phone rings.)*

TERRY. Aren't you gong to get that?

ELI. I have a service.

TERRY. But you're here.

ELI. I'm talking to you.

TERRY. I've been here when you've answered the phone. Your service isn't picking up.

ELI. They will.

TERRY. Do you know who's calling?

ELI. No.

TERRY. Do you have a suspicion?

ELI. What's your point?

TERRY. Could it be Marisa?

ELI. Why would it be her?

TERRY. Why would it? Unless it is! *(Terry grabs the phone.)* Hello? *(Listens.)* Hang up.

ELI. I have a proposition for you.

TERRY. What?

ELI. Answer my phone again and I'll reshingle the roof of your mouth.

TERRY. That's the most direct thing you've ever said to me. I stole your wife and you weren't that direct.

ELI. Nobody steals anybody's wife.

TERRY. I stole yours.

14

ELI.   She left me. She didn't even leave me. It wasn't about me anymore than it was about you.

TERRY.   Oh, it was about me. She came to me.

ELI.   We're just egomaniacs. She was living her life. We were like two trees out her train's window. Scenery. You think too much of yourself. I used to do the same thing.

TERRY.   And now?

ELI.   My insignificance has found its voice. It's like Galileo testifying, saying very softly but firmly: It's not you, chump, it's the sun. We had it wrong for so long. Tell the Pope. It's the sun.

TERRY.   You tell the Pope! What's this got to do with Marisa?

ELI.   Not much. There are stars governing Marisa no doubt, but they're not our stars. We're on our own. We can make ourselves believe that everything we do or say is about this person who isn't here and doesn't give a damn about us, or we can face up. It's just you and me, buddy. And about the one thing you're right. In effect. If I ever gave Marisa the clap and she turned around and gave it to you. And now she's gone and it's just you and me. Then forget Marisa. She was just the telephone we talked through. I gave you the clap.

TERRY.   You did?!

ELI.   No, no. Man! I am just so fucking bored with you! You're like forcing me to live in a shoe box and talk in the lint and dust about some gone away shoe. Cracks in the ceiling. What do they remind you of? Did you start off this way?

TERRY.   Now wait a minute!

ELI.   Everything boils down to something you call Marisa. Marisa? What is Marisa?

TERRY.   No. Who is Marisa!

ELI.   No! What is Marisa! Because you use this name to reduce all experience between us to like the squeakings of mice!

TERRY.   There isn't much between us anyway. I haven't got any feeling. Not really.

ELI.   How could you, buddy? You never bothered to ask who I am.

TERRY.   I know you as well as I want to.

ELI.   That's not saying much. I've always had this problem

with enthusiasm and force. I've always had this problem, when I liked somebody, that I'd grab their hand and run them down the street. But in my joy of having connected with someone, found someone, I would always run too fast, and they would fall, and I wouldn't stop fast enough, and this person of whom I had become enthused would get bloody. Would GET VERY BLOODY. And look up at me in shock. What had I done? And my reaction was always this homicidal kind of embarrassment where I just wanted to beat this person to death. UNTO DEATH! And live thereafter alone in the woods and know no one. Forget my identity. Sometimes I wish, I honestly wish, that I had never met another person. That I was raceless, nameless, that I had no rap sheet with anybody, that I did not have this blood on my hands!

TERRY.   What blood? Wait a minute! What.... Have you done something to Marisa?

ELI.   CHEESE AND RICE! WHAT'S WRONG WITH YOU?!

TERRY.   I guess not.

ELI.   This has nothing to do with your precious Marisa!

TERRY.   I just wanted to make sure.

ELI.   If you didn't know me at all. If I was a stranger and I stepped up to you and slapped your face, and didn't answer you when you asked me why, we would be further along then we are having known each other for years, slept with the same woman, etc.

TERRY.   There's something sort've infantile about that fantasy.

ELI.   Sophomoric, maybe. Not infantile.

TERRY.   It's unmodern. You're dating yourself.

ELI.   Yes, I am. I am dating myself. I'm seeing someone and it's me. It's worse if they're fat.

TERRY.   What?

ELI.   If I accidentally injure someone who's fat, that's worse.

TERRY.   Just exactly how many people have you injured?

ELI.   I don't know. That's like how many women have you slept with?

TERRY.   No, it's not.

ELI.   Well then, how many?

TERRY.   That's ...

ELI.   Do you know?

TERRY.   Exactly?

ELI.   Yes.

TERRY.   No.

ELI.   You've never sat down and figured it out?

TERRY.   No.

ELI.   Well then, why should I know how many people I've accidentally injured?

TERRY.   Actually, I do know the exact number of women I've slept with.

ELI.   You do?

TERRY.   Yeah.

ELI.   So do I, Sport, but it's none of your business.

TERRY.   Eighteen.

ELI.   Eighteen!

TERRY.   What? Is that a lot or a little?

ELI.   Compared to what? Zeus?

TERRY.   Compared to you.

ELI.   My mother told me I was going to be fat when I grew up. I think that's why I have a horror of injuring the fat. It's like savaging myself in some alternate and more vulnerable incarnation. I sliced this fat girl's knee in a head-on bicycle thing and I remember looking into her knee through this gaping slice and blood and I remember thinking: Look at that white layer of fat there. I remember thinking: That's her fat. Am I going to wear a bloody thick white coat of fat like that? Like some kind of lardy mattress pad quilting my bones about? Or for me will it be some other kind of extra useless thing? Like isolation. Will that be my unshuckable aspect of wardrobe? Terry, look at me! Where's the meat? Or is it like Marisa?

TERRY.   Marisa's not fat.

ELI.   She's not central.

TERRY.   You sound like her.

ELI.   I am not Marisa!

TERRY.   Just as dissatisfied as you are with me, that's how dissatisfied I am with you. I bet that's like a general equation you could make about any encounter between two people.

17

Unless of course ...

ELI. But what about friendship?

TERRY. What friendship?

ELI. Ours.

TERRY. You'd cut my throat if you had the shot.

ELI. There's ten things I'd do if you trusted me. Only one in ten would be the throat-cut-thing. Think of the other nine alternatives.

TERRY. You think of them.

ELI. I will. The hand clasp. Contact. If you trusted me.

TERRY. That's a paltry one.

ELI. Oh, you're counting. How rudimentary. Advice good, advice bad.

TERRY. A mere three.

ELI. Count silently. I might make you take yourself less seriously. Take me more seriously. I might educate you about a third party.

TERRY. Who?

ELI. Never mind who!

TERRY. You couldn't tell me anything about her!

ELI. I could accuse you of something.

TERRY. What?

ELI. Forgive you.

TERRY. Forgive me what?!

ELI. That's nine alternatives to cutting your throat, Terry.

TERRY. That's eight.

ELI. Oh, but who's counting?

TERRY. I am.

ELI. But who cares?

TERRY. I do.

ELI. But who are you? And what are you to me if there's no trust? No possible Renaissance. Impregnating gesture. If this is just a vignette. A handsome boy drowning in his own reflection under the supervision of a jealous moon.

TERRY. Who's the moon? You?

ELI. No, I am not the moon. I am well under the moon.

TERRY. What could you forgive me, Eli?

ELI. The fact that, potentially, you could block my reading light. But let's stop these oblique thrusts and parries.

TERRY.   That's fine with me.

ELI.   It's exhausting.

TERRY.   I wasn't doing it. It wasn't me. I try to bluntly step forward and blurt.

ELI.   Let's talk about Marisa if Marisa's what you want to talk about.

TERRY.   I don't need to talk about her.

ELI.   Let's just talk about her till there's nothing left of her.

TERRY.   I could talk about something else.

ELI.   She had big eyes.

TERRY.   I don't need to talk about this.

ELI.   She had great big eyes.

TERRY.   Yes, she did. She had great big eyes. Liquid and blue. Like spiral staircases leading down to a room, a dungeon room, a prison, my prison.

ELI.   She had great energy.

TERRY.   Yes, she did. Lots of energy.

ELI.   And a certain ability to bust your balls.

TERRY.   Well, she was a bitch.

ELI.   She had a bitchy side.

TERRY.   She was a howling bitch. She could clear a restaurant.

ELI.   I got along with her though.

TERRY.   I never did.

ELI.   I have this ability to abandon my point of view which worked pretty well with her.

TERRY.   She was sexy though. Sometimes. When the mood was on her. Like a voluptuous slinky.

ELI.   I have this ability to abandon my body, too, if necessary. And it was necessary, on occasion, with Marisa.

TERRY.   You know, I take it back. I take it all back. She wasn't a bitch. I miss her.

ELI.   That's human, and by that I mean chaotic and twisted.

TERRY.   When I told her that I had the clap, it was a very emotional scene.

ELI.   I bet.

TERRY.   She denied that she'd given it to me. She accused me! But there was no way that was going to stick. I had the bottom line fact of monogamous certainty. She burst into tears. I found myself comforting her.

ELI.   What man hasn't been that idiot.

TERRY.   Then the whole thing turned a corner. She fanned open those thighs. I was like a monkey seeing aluminum foil for the first time. From that point on, of course, she could say that I gave it to her. The clap, that is.

ELI.   Did she?

TERRY.   No. She still said she didn't have it!

ELI.   Well that's.... Then you're ... obtuse!

TERRY.   She had this position, has this position, wherever the hell she is, and she won't give it up!

ELI.   She thinks the earth's axis goes right up her dress and pops out the top of her head.

TERRY.   She should have road signs leading to her saying *this street does not go through*.

ELI.   Well. The chicken must be ready.

TERRY.   The chicken? What chicken?

ELI.   I've been baking a chicken. Let's take a look at it. *(Eli opens the oven and takes out a baked chicken.)*

TERRY.   I smelled it, but I thought it was coming in the window.

ELI.   No, it's my chicken.

TERRY.   It's big.

ELI.   Not that big.

TERRY.   C'mon. It's a roaster. Big enough for three anyway.

ELI.   Two.

TERRY.   But I thought we were just having coffee?

ELI.   We are. This is for later.

TERRY.   After I go.

ELI.   That's right.

TERRY.   Dinner for two.

ELI.   I read this book, *Bartlett's Quotations*.

TERRY.   Dinner for two.

ELI.   This guy Bartlett had an incredible mind.

TERRY.   She's coming here, isn't she?

ELI.   And he had a tremendous sensitivity to attention span. Never goes on at any length. Just a little something pithy, and moves on.

TERRY. That was her on the phone. She heard me and hung up. It was her, wasn't it?

ELI. Now Terry, what if it was?

TERRY. Was it?

ELI. Isn't she my wife?

TERRY. Hasn't the divorce gone through?

ELI. Wouldn't it be alright for her to call me?

TERRY. No.

ELI. And even if I wanted to make her dinner. Wouldn't that be alright, given that she was once my spouse?

TERRY. So the divorce has gone through.

ELI. And even if we slept together, and I had previously consoled myself with a girl of such loose habits that contracting the clap, or worse, was not out of the question. Wouldn't that be understandable?

TERRY. I can understand it.

ELI. And human?

TERRY. Yes.

ELI. And forgivable? *(Terry struggles with the question.)*

TERRY. Is that what you want from me?

ELI. Have we never been friends?

TERRY. You were married.

ELI. Yes.

TERRY. By comparison, I'm just an aging eternal boy. My quality, what was beautiful and natural about my quality, the years have made grotesque. That will always be in the way. Between us.

ELI. Make a wish, Terry.

TERRY. I wish I was alone and liked it.

ELI. Make another wish.

TERRY. I wish I was with somebody and like it.

ELI. I see you're at home with contradiction.

TERRY. Better than being home with my mother.

ELI. That's two wishes. Make it three. That's the formula. What's the third wish.

TERRY. Serve me that chicken.

ELI. Oh, ask anything of me but that, and I will prove my

friendship.

TERRY. Serve me that chicken, Eli.

ELI. I can't do that.

TERRY. I've been smelling unconsciously. It's affected me without my knowing it. I'm starving for chicken. There's enough for three. It's a roaster.

ELI. You're not thinking of the repercussions. I can't serve someone a mutilated chicken for dinner.

TERRY. Why can't we connect?

ELI. I don't know.

TERRY. I'd like to believe it's Marisa.

ELI. It's not.

TERRY. Give me some fucking chicken!

ELI. Why did you never marry?

TERRY. Why *did* you marry?

ELI. I wanted a home!

TERRY. *I* have a home!

ELI. I wanted children.

TERRY. You don't have children!

ELI. I *thought* I wanted children!

TERRY. I've had bastards.

ELI. I wanted love.

TERRY. You wanted Marisa.

ELI. I did want Marisa.

TERRY. Did you get love?

ELI. Some. Not enough. A ration. A half ration.

TERRY. What do you know about getting by on very little?! I'm the expert on starvation! Now. If you pick a small piece of meat off the bird's bottom — there's two little pockets of dark meat under there — if you do that, no one would every know.

ELI. No.

TERRY. Please.

ELI. No.

TERRY. Please.

ELI. No.

TERRY. Please, please, please!

ELI. Alright, alright. (*Eli carefully spoons a small piece of meat from under the bird.)*

TERRY.   Be careful to leave no trace. Slide the skin back. Use a spoon.

ELI.   "The flea, though he cannot kill, does all the harm he can."

TERRY.   What are you talking about?

ELI.   That's Bartlett!

TERRY.   "Nothing emboldens sin so much as mercy." That's Shakespeare.

ELI.   No, that's Bartlett, too. But everybody stole from him. Alright, blow on it. It's hot. *(Terry blows on it repeatedly.)*

TERRY.   I'm getting dizzy.

ELI.   The earth's rotation will do that. Eat. *Mangé.*

TERRY.   And when I eat this, and when I eat this, and when I eat this, and when I eat this, and when I eat this ...

ELI.   Oh, would you eat it before the sun goes down on us! *(Terry eats.)* What do you think?

TERRY.   It's good.

ELI.   You think so.

TERRY.   It's moist.

ELI.   That's what I was after.

TERRY.   It is good! Was this a chicken that had a good life?

ELI.   As a matter of fact, this was a chicken.... Oh, he was the Richard Cory of chickens. Charismatic, androgenous, a dance captain's posture of authority. But then he became despondent, went in the coop. There was a shot.

TERRY.   When will they give us gun control?

ELI.   Everyone was shocked. Not that chicken. Nobody could believe it.

TERRY.   Maybe he knew Marisa? *(Savage laughter from both.)*

ELI.   Oh, maybe he did! I'm glad we've got a sense of humor about it. At last.

TERRY.   Oh, I see the humor in too many things. Privation does that to a man. I see the humor in the mirror.

ELI.   You're like a skeleton!

TERRY.   That's it! I'm like a rattling around skeleton, rattling around, grinning, hoping if not to frighten then at least amuse.

23

ELI. Oh, you frighten me.

TERRY. Do I? What is it? Is it my ruined youth?

ELI. No.

TERRY. The absence of future from my squeeze-toy heart?

ELI. No.

TERRY. How much I've stolen from you, beaten you, circumvented you, forced you into emotional perjury?

ELI. No, it's none of those things, my friend.

TERRY. Do you fear that I'll take Marisa away from you again?

ELI. There is no Marisa. *(Terry takes up a knife.)*

TERRY. Tell me! What is it about me frightens you? Am I missing my own greatness? Are you drawfed by my grand good fortune that I cannot know? Am I deaf to my own poetry, afraid of my courage, numb to my own fine feelings? Or am I dangerous to you in the old original way? Are you terrified that I may replace you, kill you, that I am your murdering twin?! Or is it that I'm an animal! Just an animal. And so revolt your basic humanity? Is it because I wear makeup? Just a little. To hold off the inevitable a few more days. I remember when we were equals.

ELI. Yes. I remember when we thought we were equals.

TERRY. I remember when my terror did not outweigh my optimism.

ELI. I remember when I was optimistic about you. But then, then, you were truly young.

TERRY. What about me could possibly frighten you, old comrade?

ELI. That look of hope in your eyes. Your hope.

TERRY. Alright. I am failing at life.

ELI. No. Don't say that.

TERRY. I am failing at life, and you are not.

ELI. Terry, I'm sorry.

TERRY. Eli, in this brief moment before my guardians close rank around me for the remainder of my days, I forgive you.

ELI. Why?

TERRY. For the sake of friendship. We were friends back before the forking of the road. And for the sake of the ghostly gossamer Marisa, who softened my hatred of you, and eased my love.

ELI.   Thank you.

TERRY.   It's the least I can do. The chicken, the little I am allowed, was very, very good.

ELI.   You're welcome.

TERRY.   I am welcome nowhere.

THE END

PROPERTY LIST

Cups of coffee (TERRY, ELI)
Baked chicken (ELI)
Knife (TERRY)

SOUND EFFECTS

Phone ring

KISSING CHRISTINE

KISSING CHRISTINE

Larry and Christine are eating in a Thai restaurant severely influenced by Tibet. Behind them is a big Tibetan Buddha with many hands. They're sitting at one of those low tables, in chairs without legs.

They're eating with chopsticks. They have beers. They're nicely dressed. He sports hair tonic. She has a little bow in her hair.

At rise, they're eating soup.

LARRY. Yummy.

CHRISTINE. Have you been here before?

LARRY. What? Excuse me. No. I picked it out of a magazine. This little ad.

CHRISTINE. It's quite a production really. The decor.

LARRY. Yeah. The Buddha. It's you, me, and the Buddha.

CHRISTINE. One, two, three. Isn't three supposed to be a dynamic number?

LARRY. Incomplete. Waiting for the fourth.

CHRISTINE. The visiting mystery. The uninvited guest.

LARRY. He certainly has a lot of hands.

CHRISTINE. I've been on dates like that. *(Pause.)*

LARRY. Single. Singleness. What is 'single'?

CHRISTINE. You mean like, I'm single? As opposed to married or significantly entangled?

LARRY. Beer.

CHRISTINE. Isn't beer beautiful? The way the bubbles come from points of nothing.

LARRY. Yeah.

CHRISTINE. Door to another world.

LARRY. The bubble world.

CHRISTINE. There are different kinds of intelligence.

LARRY. Sure.

CHRISTINE.   What kind am I?

LARRY.   Quick.

CHRISTINE.   I'm quick?

LARRY.   That's the gloss anyway. Under that is something quite different again. You're, you know, the actual way you are. There's the gloss, which really probably reflects back aspects that are coming at you. Right now: me. Like you're a fielder. Dealing with the balls that come under way. And you're a quick fielder. You're good. But under that, the other kind of intelligence, that's when you're at bat. And you're the pitcher. And the ball.

CHRISTINE.   You know, originally I'm from Queens.

LARRY.   I didn't know that.

CHRISTINE.   Yeah. So that part of me wants to say, "What the fuck are you talking about?!"

LARRY.   I'm talking about whatever comes into my head.

CHRISTINE.   I know. And another part of me wants to have this kind of conversation because it's different from when I grew up, WHICH WAS STULTIFYING! You know, I lived with a guy, he knew me like a book. If I needed a pillow behind me in my chair when I sat down, he had the pillow there. He knew my thoughts. He knew my music. He could work me like the bar sharpie works the shuffleboard machine. Do you know what that's like?

LARRY.   I think it'd give me the creeps.

CHRISTINE.   No. It's pretty nice. It's very complete. It has a lot of good points.

LARRY.   So what happened?

CHRISTINE.   I left him.

LARRY.   Why?

CHRISTINE.   I was getting bored. I was starting to feel sadistic.

LARRY.   You don't mean sadistic.

CHRISTINE.   Alright, what do I mean?

LARRY.   I don't know.

CHRISTINE.   Did you ever have an event, a single event, that changed everything like that?!

LARRY.   Well, I'm sure I have, but.... I mean I'm sure I've had a few ...

CHRISTINE.   I fell in a hole.

LARRY.   You fell.... You what?

CHRISTINE.   I fell in a hole. I was in a deli. I turned a corner. There was nothing there. It was a hole. And I fell in.

LARRY.   There was a hole in a deli?

CHRISTINE.   It was a trapdoor in the floor. Somebody left it open. It was late. I fell through. I fell fifteen feet. Landed on my head. Got a bad concussion. Messed up my face.

LARRY.   Really.

CHRISTINE.   I was paralyzed for six months.

LARRY.   Jesus.

CHRISTINE.   When I could walk again, and after the reconstructive surgery, and after the speech therapy ...

LARRY.   What did you need that for?

CHRISTINE.   I forgot how to talk. My brain was affected.

LARRY.   So you were like completely destroyed.

CHRISTINE.   Yeah. My speech therapist was from the Midwest so now I have a slight Midwest accent. I lost my Queens accent while I was still in Queens. And my face. I used to have a round face. Now it's long.

LARRY.   I don't know what to say.

CHRISTINE.   You want to hear the strangest thing?

LARRY.   What?

CHRISTINE.   I used to be.... I used to have a different personality.

LARRY.   What do you mean?

CHRISTINE.   I lot of people who knew me before have commented on it. Even my mother says it's true.

LARRY.   You mean the experienced changed you.

CHRISTINE.   I mean I got hit on the head and before that I was different than I was after.

LARRY.   What were you like?

CHRISTINE.   Oh, I was sly, you know? Always looking for the opportunity to slip in the knife. Always had something to say. And I had this very specific laugh. You know, the kind of laugh that runs up a bill and somebody has to pay. I was cruel.

LARRY.   So you looked different and you talked different and you *were* different.

CHRISTINE.   Yes.

LARRY.   How long ago did this happen?

CHRISTINE.   Little over three years ago.

LARRY.   Three again.

CHRISTINE.   Unstable number.

LARRY.   You know I invited you to dinner, I thought it might be fun to go out and get to know each other a little bit ...

CHRISTINE.   Me too.

LARRY.   I wish you were going to have amnesia tomorrow.

CHRISTINE.   Why? Do you have a secret?

LARRY.   Sure. Why did you tell me?

CHRISTINE.   I felt you were starting to assume a huge number of things about me that weren't true, and before you dug yourself in too deep.... Anyway, a revelation's always fun, right?

LARRY.   Your face is so beautiful. I can't imagine that it was ever damaged.

CHRISTINE.   All that stuff, it's not that important.

LARRY.   What is important?

CHRISTINE.   Nothing.

LARRY.   What did you say?

CHRISTINE.   You asked me what's important. I can't think of anything.

LARRY.   I can.

CHRISTINE.   What?

LARRY.   I think it's important that this minute I can't remember your name.

CHRISTINE.   It's Christine.

LARRY.   Of course it's Christine. How could that have happened, how could I have forgotten?

CHRISTINE.   And your name's Larry.

LARRY.   I remembered my name. What you're saying disturbs me very much.

CHRISTINE.   What did I say?

LARRY.   Nothing's important.

CHRISTINE.   Oh don't let me bother you. Just forget it.

LARRY.   It upsets me because I find myself in agreement.

CHRISTINE.   You don't think anything's important either?

LARRY.   Why couldn't I remember your name?!

CHRISTINE.   I'm not offended.

LARRY.   It's just, I mean, I find it strange. That's not like me!

CHRISTINE.   We've only known each other.... We don't know each other.

LARRY.   But to ask a woman on a ... and not be able to remember her *name?!* I've never had that experience. Before.

CHRISTINE.   Good.

LARRY.   But that's not like me.

CHRISTINE.   Think of my situation. Everything I do is not like me. I've become very comfortable with that. Larry.

LARRY.   I just, I'm, I, it's, not to be melodramatic but.... Married.

CHRISTINE.   Married. You're married.

LARRY.   Yes.

CHRISTINE.   You're married.

LARRY.   Yes.

CHRISTINE.   You didn't tell me that.

LARRY.   No. I neglected ...

CHRISTINE.   Well. And you asked me on a date.

LARRY.   Yes.

CHRISTINE.   And your wife is where?

LARRY.   Home.

CHRISTINE.   *(Simultaneous.)* Home.

LARRY.   I'm sorry.

CHRISTINE.   You're sorry what? You're sorry that you're married?

LARRY.   Yes. Naw, I'm sorry that I've been duplicitous.

CHRISTINE.   To me?

LARRY.   Yes.

CHRISTINE.   To your wife?

LARRY.   Yes.

CHRISTINE.   To yourself?

LARRY.   Yes.

CHRISTINE.   So you're REALLY sorry.

LARRY.   I don't know what to do.

CHRISTINE.   Eat something.

LARRY. I really don't know what to do.

CHRISTINE. I feel sorry for all men.

LARRY. That's nice. Why?

CHRISTINE. They suffer like dumb beasts.

LARRY. Yeah. So, you're alone.

CHRISTINE. That's right. I'm single.

LARRY. Single. Singleness. What is single?

CHRISTINE. Being single is mysterious. It's silent. You live large parts of your life unobserved. There's no one there saying, That's the third time you've gone to the bathroom. Why do you laugh like that? Are you going to do anything today? There's no one there saying, You look unhappy. What is it? I find for myself that when I live with someone, my life lacks depth. It has scope, it has activity…. I don't know what I'm trying to say. Single, married, both ways are hard. Sometimes you want to suffer and not be seen. Then it's better to be single. Sometimes you don't even suffer unless there's someone there seeing you. Then it's much better to be single. It's better to be married when it's better to be married. For a woman, it's great when you're checking into a hotel and you're Mrs. Whatever. A very solid feeling I can only imagine.

LARRY. What about children?

CHRISTINE. That's more than I know about. I don't have children.

LARRY. I do. Two girls. The twins.

CHRISTINE. Look, Larry, why don't you just go home.

LARRY. I can't go home. I've lost my dignity. If I say I'm upset, my wife says she's more upset. If I say, I'm scared. She says she's terrified. Whatever I am, she's more, so I must be less. I am diminished. I am vanishing.

CHRISTINE. That's a lot.

LARRY. And why couldn't I remember your name?

CHRISTINE. Maybe my name isn't important.

LARRY. Oh, I just ate a whole hot pepper! Wow! Boy, that's hot!

CHRISTINE. Have some water.

LARRY. She's not bad, my wife, I just want her to disappear.

CHRISTINE. What about the kids?

LARRY.   Oh, I love them but I can't take care of them, I don't want to take care of them, but if I didn't see them, I would miss them right away. Right away. They're beautiful.

CHRISTINE.   You can't control your nature.

LARRY.   I know. That's what scares the shit out of me. Like you. You fell in a hole. It's like that.

CHRISTINE.   So here we are.

LARRY.   Right. Sitting on the floor, Thai food. I like this.

CHRISTINE.   Having a conversation.

LARRY.   Having a truthful conversation. Truth and spicy food go together in the sense that they both make me sweat.

CHRISTINE.   The truth can be used as a spice. But that's perhaps ...

LARRY.   So this guy you left, the one who could read your every mood, were you with him before or after you fell in the hole?

CHRISTINE.   After.

LARRY.   Was your relationship, did it have a feeling like he was your nurse?

CHRISTINE.   Yeah.

LARRY.   Were you still messed up when he met you?

CHRISTINE.   Not so you could see.

LARRY.   Are you still messed up now?

CHRISTINE.   Yes.

LARRY.   You are?

CHRISTINE.   Yes.

LARRY.   How? Do you know?

CHRISTINE.   I don't know. I just know something's still wrong.

LARRY.   Before I was married, I was a different person.

CHRISTINE.   What were you like?

LARRY.   I don't know. I couldn't tell you what I'm currently like, no matter what I was like in some bygone time slot. So what were you doing at that meeting?

CHRISTINE.   I saw a flyer by a phone in a restaurant and I wrote down the number. I don't know why. I think I must have felt the subject was so specifically esoteric that, well, it made me curious.

LARRY.   I picked up a leaflet in a Jungian bookstore.

CHRISTINE.   I didn't even know there was such a thing as a Jungian bookstore.

LARRY.   You're kidding. I know of two purely Jungian bookstores. And several Jung, slash, flako, occult, Dolphins-are-citizens-of-Atlantis bookstores.

CHRISTINE.   New York.

LARRY.   New York, Seattle, LA, Boulder. What did you think of the lecture?

CHRISTINE.   Well, I thought she was a little heavy.

LARRY.   She made some witty comments.

CHRISTINE.   I mean her weight. She was fat.

LARRY.   Oh. Yeah.

CHRISTINE.   So I thought, what does she know? She can't even diet. A dancer's prejudice. But then I thought she started to make some very good points. I didn't understand the box with the numbers.

LARRY.   The Chinese Divination Box.

CHRISTINE.   Yeah.

LARRY.   I felt I understood that while she was explaining it, but I didn't take away an understanding.

CHRISTINE.   What a subject. The Study of Meaningful Chance. I think the most amazing thing about the lecture is that I went.

LARRY.   I've never gone to anything like that before. You were a dancer?

CHRISTINE.   Oh God!

LARRY.   What?

CHRISTINE.   Oh my God!

LARRY.   What?

CHRISTINE.   Peppers!

LARRY.   You mean the —

CHRISTINE.   I ate one of those peppers! Oh my God they're hot!

LARRY.   It's the shriveled ones. There's about ten of them. Have some water.

CHRISTINE.   Thanks. It's hard to believe people think of that as a seasoning. I mean, my lip is numb.

LARRY.   Should I ask the server to do something with it?

CHRISTINE.   No, no. I accept my fate. Even if I don't always relish it.

LARRY.   I have a very strong fate.

CHRISTINE.   What do you mean by that?

LARRY.   The whole world tells me what to do. Not people. Not in the social sense. The whole living world. Strangers are part of that. Strangers saying things to you that have meaning for you. Signs. Scraps of newspaper. A drop of water hitting you on the head in a very particular way that makes you feel the presence of meaning.

CHRISTINE.   Did you read *The Celestine Prophecy?*

LARRY.   Yeah. Total bullshit. Nancy Drew goes to Peru.

CHRISTINE.   I couldn't put it down.

LARRY.   Me neither. Basically, the guy's a paranoid. It's just that he's a positive paranoid. He writes positive conspiracy theories. Those guys can flip though. Those guys have a tendency to flip. Cat Stevens? The trick is to start from an experience that people have had, getting them nodding, saying, Yeah, that's happened to me, and then take them, walk them, talk them to some Egyptian, Sci-Fi, flako, occult, Dolphins-are-registered-to-vote-in-Atlantis scenario. That's not to say I haven't had a psychic experience.

CHRISTINE.   I've had them. But I've only had them when I wasn't trying to have them. Oh, there's my lip. Feeling has returned.

LARRY.   What am I going to do about my life?

CHRISTINE.   Are things bad?

LARRY.   Things are bad. Things are very bad. My life has stopped working. It's only a matter of time before I stop working.

CHRISTINE.   Did you read about the cop who talked a guy out of committing suicide and then committed suicide himself?

LARRY.   I did read about that! Why would he do that?

CHRISTINE.   It's like he made a deal with Death.

LARRY.   I feel like there was a period when there was a lot of stories like that. Deals with Death or the Devil. And the importance of talk.

CHRISTINE. Right. Like the Devil and Daniel Webster.

LARRY. Yeah, that kind of thing! There were all these things about the power of talking. Daniel Webster can save your life by out-talking the Devil.

CHRISTINE. Cyrano can talk and make a woman fall in love with you.

LARRY. *Inherit the Wind.* You can turn a bunch of yahoos around. Clarence Darrow.

CHRISTINE. Right, right. And Brutus was an honorable man.

LARRY. Maybe he was. But Marc Antony had the microphone.

CHRISTINE. That cop made a speech and turned a man around from taking his own life.

LARRY. Paid a big price.

CHRISTINE. Yes. Do you believe that somebody could say something to you that would make your whole life better or work or improve in some important way?

LARRY. Yes.

CHRISTINE. What could someone say to you?

LARRY. I don't know. Exactly what I haven't thought of, I guess.

CHRISTINE. After my accident, when I was lying paralyzed for six months, I had a lot of time to think. I thought about all the cruel things I'd done in my life. I tried to remember every generous thing I'd ever done. Moments of insight, of terrible pain, of pleasure. I tried to see patterns, the patterns in my lists. I saw some things. I made some connections. But after a while it all began to dissolve away like a lace cookie dissolves away in your mouth. Some sweetness, then all gone like a dream. At first it felt like I was wearing an iron hat that was just a little too small. That was the concussion. My brain was actually swollen, pressing against my skull. After a time, that lessened. The feeling of the hat. But I could feel myself then like a tiny object caught in a great flood. I still have that feeling. Like I'm bound up, a little splinter pitching along in a black rush. People said I was different after the accident. That the blow to my head had hurt me. Maybe. Six months to think about things changed me. Banging my brain changed me. But I look at people and people change. Don't you agree?

LARRY. Sometimes. Most of the time, no. I don't know.

CHRISTINE. People change. People do. I mean think of evolution. We crawled up out of the sea. We rejected life underwater. It's just that nobody notices. I noticed my change. It had a sudden look. People were looking to see if I'd been affected and I had been. And they shook their heads, my own mother shook her head and said, Christine has changed.

LARRY. What am I going to do about my life?

CHRISTINE. I don't know, Larry.

LARRY. I know it's a terrible thing to say, but I wish in a way that I had fallen in a hole, and that everybody knew to expect that I was going to be different afterwards.

CHRISTINE. Why was that woman fat, do you think?

LARRY. You mean the woman who gave the lecture?

CHRISTINE. Yeah.

LARRY. She probably sits around reading her books and talking to people on the phone and, you know, she's sedentary and ... she eats.

CHRISTINE. Yeah. She eats.

LARRY. This is the fattest country in the world.

CHRISTINE. Think of that. It's like she lost her body. Traded it in. She went through that point of nothing into the bubble world. I'm sorry. I don't know what I'm doing.

LARRY. You are like, in the realm of ideas.

CHRISTINE. And you are like, where?

LARRY. Me? I'm just drowning in reality.

CHRISTINE. You're fine.

LARRY. No, I'm not.

CHRISTINE. Alright, you're not.

LARRY. I can't blame you for not immediately understanding. It's funny how the circumstances of your life can build up. You have kids. That's one change. I mean, you already had one change. You got married. Now you lay on top of that: kids. A couple acts of faith and you're in a whole new place. A different place. It isn't just you anymore. You're a family. You have kids, there's no time. You've got to give up everything. You can't read, talk on the phone, stay up late, have a conversation like this. It's a lot.

CHRISTINE. Yes.

LARRY. You're a family. Try seeing that in the mirror. And on the partner front, this woman you hooked up with transmutates into a wife and a mother, and you revolve into the role of schmuck. You walk in the door and she is like in a righteous rage and you are like wrong. Name a subject. She is right and you are wrong. She's looking at you like she hates you. To be a man in this situation is.... Everything is a destroyed version of something that was good. Your rules are like cracked bells that used to ring so true. Your love life is gutted. Your finer feelings.... You don't have any finer feelings. You have these electric shredded wires picking up this continuous unanswerable stream of blame. Your life, MY LIFE — let me not divorce myself from my own LIFE — has become a stupid contest of pain with my wife. And I would let her win if I knew how. Anything to end it. Give me something to sign, give me something to say. I'll sign it, I'll say it. But it's not to be. We're like enemies who fell off a cliff fighting, and we're gonna strangle each other all the way down. You should see her. You should see the way she is. Did I do this to her? She says I did. If I did, and there's a Hell, they will put me there. *(A Server, a lovely woman in Tibetan-Thai attire, appears, smiling. The two diners notice her and fall silent. They smile, as if on cue, after a moment.)*

SERVER. Hiii. How are you doing today? Okay?

CHRISTINE. Good.

LARRY. Very good. Fine.

SERVER. Just back from my break. Need anything?

LARRY. No, thank you.

SERVER. More beer? More water?

LARRY. Actually.

CHRISTINE. I would have another beer.

LARRY. Me too.

SERVER. And why not let down your guard and have the water, too? After all, it's free.

LARRY. That's true.

CHRISTINE.   Actually, I'd love some water.

SERVER.   Good. The best things in life are free, right?

CHRISTINE.   Right.

LARRY.   Yeah.

SERVER.   The best people in life are free, right?

CHRISTINE.   True.

LARRY.   That is probably true.

SERVER.   Easy to say, but to remember, that's the trick. Try this on. Can you really remember this candle?

LARRY.   Excuse me?

SERVER.   We have to be here, now, the three of us and the candle burning to have the experience. When this light goes out and we go our separate ways, can you really remember this candle? Think about it. Of course sometimes memory's all you have. That's all I have left of my mother. My mother used to say, you want water around. You have water around, everything is going to be okay. That's why I was pushing the water. Are you okay?

LARRY.   I'm alright.

SERVER.   But there's bad news, too.

CHRISTINE.   There is?

SERVER.   Oh, there's always the balancing bad news. The bad news on the water front is that my sister lives in the desert.

CHRISTINE.   Oh, so …

SERVER.   No water. Her boyfriend took her there. Nevada. She called me this morning. She's using like a gallon of moisturizer a day! Here's a picture of her. Look at those sunglasses! What's she doing out there? Welding?

LARRY.   Nice looking girl.

SERVER.   Nice looking girl. I told her she's sweet, I told her she's good, I told her she should come and work with me. But the manager here's a strange man. He keeps going up on the roof. I think he's on drugs. He's Portuguese. He smells like a sardine. And he's got these little folds around his mouth …

CHRISTINE.   Excuse me! Enough!

SERVER.   Two beers.

CHRISTINE.   Thanks.

SERVER.   *(Muttering.)* He better not try anything with me. He

better not try anything with me all night. *(The server goes.)*
CHRISTINE.   Thank you.
LARRY.   Thank you. *(To Christine.)* Well. Where were we?
CHRISTINE.   Who knows? I can't tell you how many times that's happened to me.
LARRY.   What?
CHRISTINE.   Somebody shows up like…. The Annunciation. And then they start bitching about the Portuguese.
LARRY.   I have an idea about that.
CHRISTINE.   You do?
LARRY.   All these gods. There used to be all these gods. And they used to impersonate people. Odysseus arrives home and Athena impersonates a guy he knows. Nestor. Odysseus runs into he thinks Nestor, who tells him something he needs to know. He goes on his way. He thinks he talked to Nestor. But he wasn't talking to Nestor. He was talking to a god inhabiting the appearance of Nestor. He was talking to a god. And you recognize it. I've seen it. You're taking to a woman, a woman you know, you've known her forever. And one night, you see her, look into her face. The Goddess of Love. The eyes, the skin, the hair, the Goddess of Love. You kiss her. It's like tumbling down a wild Irish mountain and the wolves are howling and stars are crashing into the earth. But the next day, the next minute sometimes, it's just a woman again. The Goddess has fled. Gone into some other girl. Or hidden her light beneath the ocean or something. Or she starts bitching about the Portuguese. I've felt it in myself. Moments when I give over to something else. A natural, sudden certainty of bravery, or romantic love, or mental clearness. And afterwards I think, that was Ares, or Aphrodite, or grey-eyed Athena. Never at the time. Always afterwards. A truly peculiar delightful feeling of humility. Of who was that man? It is sort've a Lone Ranger feeling. Who was that man, that mask? Who did that deed that needed to be done? And I think, why it was a god. They're hiding. They're still here. Just like they always were. So you work in publishing.
CHRISTINE.   What? No. I'm a receptive, excuse me, a receptionist in a thing they call an Executive Tower in Long Is-

land City. And I'm a proofreader for an obscure financial newspaper on Wall Street. And you? I know you work in an office ...

LARRY.   You know what I used to be?

CHRISTINE.   What?

LARRY.   I used to be a bond salesman.

CHRISTINE.   That's...?

LARRY.   A financial instrument. I was the guy who handled the old ladies. Old ladies love bonds.

CHRISTINE.   They do?

LARRY.   Yes. I made a lot of money doing that for a while. A lot of money. That's when I met my wife. She was married to a commodities trader from Chicago who I knew. We used to have drinks when they came to New York at Christmas.

CHRISTINE.   You stole the guy's wife?

LARRY.   No. When he stopped drinking it turned out that the reason he was drinking was he was gay.

CHRISTINE.   Oh.

LARRY.   He stayed in Chicago, she moved to New York. She was still only twenty-five. We started going out.... While we were still going out, this thing happened that's always haunted me. I'm ashamed about it.

CHRISTINE.   You don't want to go home, do you?

LARRY.   This customer, bonds you know, her husband was dead. She was one of those women with nothing to do but rearrange her portfolio. She was a very good customer. She invited me to the Caribbean, old San Juan. I was seeing Babette. And I went. Babette knew about it. And I went with this fifty-five-year-old fur coat — I didn't sleep with her. But I went with her. The place where we were at had this little casino filled with only other women like her. They had these handbags stuffed with chips. And this woman, this customer, she towed me in there. See I was a trophy. And my wife, Babette, she wasn't my wife then, but my wife Babette, that was alright with her. Because it was a customer. Whenever I hear the word 'sleazy' I think about those women, that casino, their handbags croaked open with chips. I don't think a god was co-starring with me then. I don't think there's a god of sleaze.

CHRISTINE.   There's the Devil.

LARRY.   You think there's a devil?

CHRISTINE.   I think you're doing things.

LARRY.   Who said otherwise?

CHRISTINE.   You're driving the car.

LARRY.   Well, what d'you mean?

CHRISTINE.   There's something about the way you see things, it's …

LARRY.   Overblown?

CHRISTINE.   If every great moment in your life, if the way you see it is, it wasn't you that was doing it, then what are you going to think of yourself? You're left with the sleaze, and the gods did everything else.

LARRY.   Huh. I still think that's the way it is. Jesus!

CHRISTINE.   What?

LARRY.   I must be cracking up. I've forgotten your name again!

CHRISTINE.   Christine.

LARRY.   Christine. Christine. Beautiful name.

CHRISTINE.   Thank you.

LARRY.   You're a proofreader.

CHRISTINE.   Yeah.

LARRY.   And a receptionist in an executive tower.

CHRISTINE.   In Long Island City. Very good. Listen carefully. I don't really give a shit if you can remember my name. I don't really care if you can remember my face tomorrow. What does it matter? I'm your company for this meal. This conversation.

LARRY.   Okay. So I bought an apartment and I paid off the mortgage and Babette got pregnant and I quit my bond job and I got a thing selling memberships at a Greenwich Village Health Club.

CHRISTINE.   You bailed out on me!

LARRY.   What? No!

CHRISTINE.   Yes. Why are you telling me all this … garbage?

LARRY.   I don't know. Because it's my life.

CHRISTINE.   No. I feel like you're just telling me THINGS.

LARRY. Alright, let's talk about you.

CHRISTINE. I'm not interested in that, either.

LARRY. Well, what are you interested in?

CHRISTINE. Nothing.

LARRY. Nothing?

CHRISTINE. I have a burning interest in nothing. *(The Server appears with the tray of beverages.)*

SERVER. Stop the clock. *(Sings.)* I dream of Jeannie with the light brown hair. Beer, beer.

LARRY. *Spiseba.* That's Russian for thanks.

CHRISTINE. Thanks.

SERVER. You want new glasses for your beer?

CHRISTINE. We can use the ones we have. *Spiseba.*

SERVER. You're not finished with anything, are you?

CHRISTINE. No.

SERVER. Listen. I feel bad about what I said about the manager. I want to take it back. Can I take it back?

LARRY. Sure.

SERVER. Thanks. You were talking, that's good. A lot of times people sit here and they don't talk to each other. It's a tragedy. Put a little light on the subject. *(Puts another candle on their table.)* Need anything else right now?

CHRISTINE. No.

LARRY. Tea. Hot tea.

CHRISTINE. Oh, I'll have tea.

SERVER. Hot?

CHRISTINE. Yeah.

SERVER. *(Sings.)* I dream of Jeannie with the light brown hair. *(Finishes singing.)* Start the clock. *(The Server goes.)*

LARRY. She's a character.

CHRISTINE. I am not distracted. I will not be distracted. Listen. For a while there I got you were really telling me something, but then I felt you were just mindlessly dredging up dead information and dumping it on me. Now I don't mind, NO, I'm grateful for when you or anybody actually speaks to me, but I will not just be a garbage can while you automatically dispose.

LARRY. I'm sorry if I crossed some line of yours.

47

CHRISTINE. And don't appease me. You can't appease me.

LARRY. I'm trying to get along with you.

CHRISTINE. You've gone on automatic pilot and you're trying to put me in a certain box.

LARRY. I am not.

CHRISTINE. I am not your wife.

LARRY. I know you are not my wife.

CHRISTINE. Good. Nor am I the whore with a heart of gold rubbing your feet while you bitch about your wife.

LARRY. Who said anything like that?

CHRISTINE. I am reminded of that sculpture, the Pieta. The wounded man, the nurturing woman.

LARRY. As I recall, the man was dead.

CHRISTINE. Point taken, and so what?

LARRY. You're a receptionist and a proofreader?

CHRISTINE. So?

LARRY. You're too smart to be a receptionist and a proofreader.

CHRISTINE. Oh, those ideas don't apply anymore, don't you know that? There are incredibly educated people all over this city doing unbelievably strange tiny things to get by.

LARRY. I want to cry.

CHRISTINE. So cry. I didn't mean to say it that way, but why not cry?

LARRY. I can't.

CHRISTINE. Why not?

LARRY. Oh, I don't know. It's not safe.

CHRISTINE. I'm sorry I've been, I don't know how to put it, repulsing you.

LARRY. You don't repulse me.

CHRISTINE. I didn't mean it like that.

LARRY. I like you.

CHRISTINE. I was a double major in college. Philosophy and Dance. I was a dancer till I was injured. I couldn't be after that. *(The Server returns. She's wearing a coat.)*

SERVER. *(Interrupts.)* Hot tea. Hot tea.

LARRY. Why is it dark like that?

SERVER. It's Thai tea. It's different. You can't see to the

bottom. You put this sweet milk in it. It's good. Anything new's scary at first but, my friends, how scary can you be of a cup of tea? May I give you your check? I'm going home.

LARRY.   Sure. *(She puts the check on the table.)*

SERVER.   There's no hurry to pay. The man up front will take it whenever you want. Take your time. Talk forever. *(The Server goes. Christine says after her.)*

CHRISTINE.   Goodnight. *(Christine looks after the departed Server. Larry looks at Christine. Neither of them move for a long time. Then Larry reaches over, pulls Christine gently but firmly to him in a single motion, and kisses her. She is not surprised. She kisses him back. He suddenly stops the kiss.)* What is it?

LARRY.   I just got a little nervous.

CHRISTINE.   What do you need?

LARRY.   I wouldn't know where to begin.

CHRISTINE.   Because if you told me what you needed, you might get it.

LARRY.   I need to be accepted completely.

CHRISTINE.   This table accepts you completely.

LARRY.   Oh look, forget it. I'm just a ridiculous person. My problems are ridiculous and boring TO ME!

CHRISTINE.   You're unhappy.

LARRY.   Yeah.

CHRISTINE.   Why did you kiss me?

LARRY.   I couldn't think of anything else to do. *(She looks at him. She leans over and she kisses him.)*

CHRISTINE.   Your lips are soft.

LARRY.   I'm upset.

CHRISTINE.   You're scared.

LARRY.   Yeah.

CHRISTINE.   So what. It's alright.

LARRY.   What are you thinking about?

CHRISTINE.   I was thinking about, what am I going to do in my life now.

LARRY.   Don't worry. I'm not going to make some kind of demand on you.

CHRISTINE.   I wasn't thinking about you. You're like a dream to me. This restaurant is like a dream to me. I was thinking about my life. My experience. It's extremely difficult for me to really know you're here. I know you're married. You're unhappy. You've gotten into appeasing your wife, who can't be appeased. You're a man, whatever that is. Men are so different. My father was a man. He's dead. When men died, women used to wash them. I wish I'd washed my father's dead body. Been allowed that tenderness. I think it would be easier to express physical tenderness to a dead man than any man I've ever dated. You're an interesting man, Larry.

LARRY.   Me?

CHRISTINE.   Yeah.

LARRY.   I don't feel interesting. What do you find interesting about me?

CHRISTINE.   Your kiss. I felt something in my bowels when I kissed you.

LARRY.   In your bowels?

CHRISTINE.   Yeah.

LARRY.   Wow, that's … I guess that's really something. I don't know what I feel. I'm upset. Let me try this tea. So I didn't tell you what I do now for a living.

CHRISTINE.   You're a trip. I thought you sold memberships in a health club.

LARRY.   No, I quit that job. You know, I…. This is how I quit it. A guy came in, an old man. He had high blood pressure and his doctor had said, join a gym. So I was giving him my spiel about the place and he looked at me. He had these penetrating eyes, almost like he was surprised to see me there, and very surprised by what I was telling him. And right in the middle of my pitch, he blurted: What are you doing here?! And I went to answer him, it seemed so obvious, I had this job and I was doing my job, but I couldn't answer him. I didn't know why I was there. I didn't know. He made me see myself in my situation because he had this incredulity.

CHRISTINE.   You are nervous.

LARRY.   So I quit that job.

CHRISTINE.   You're a salesman.

LARRY.   Not now.

CHRISTINE.   I think I could be a very good salesman except there's nothing I believe in.

LARRY.   Now I'm running the New York office of an arts colony in Italy. They're going to do a play on a mountaintop in Umbria next August.

CHRISTINE.   Why?

LARRY.   Because this guy, he's actually a big baker here in New York, he got this vision of doing this project in Italy, he's Italian, and he's raising the money. He's raised a lot of it already.

CHRISTINE.   What do you mean, he's a big baker?

LARRY.   He bakes. He's got like five bakeries in and around New York. He's very successful. He does the cakes for all the biggest society people. He's very well connected. But, well, he's an artist. I mean if you saw the way that he decorated these cakes it would remove any doubt from your mind. And he was frustrated because it wasn't enough.

CHRISTINE.   Making cakes.

LARRY.   The whole baking thing, it didn't satisfy the artist in him, so he got this idea of starting an arts colony in this ancient Etruscan town on a mountain in Umbria, and he started a New York office to coordinate the fundraising.... See, he was the old man! Who came to gym. And asked me why I was there! His doctor said he had high blood pressure and he realized he wasn't going to live forever, and that if he was going to ever make his dream a reality, it had to be now!

CHRISTINE.   What does your wife think of this?

LARRY.   Well, it's a finite job. It ends when the colony cranks up. Or at best it's seasonal. And it doesn't pay much. I've had to take out a loan against the apartment to pay tuition. Two daughters in school. My wife thinks everything I've done for the last several cycles has been the wrong thing.

CHRISTINE.   Why doesn't she leave you?

LARRY.   She can't leave me. We're chained together like galley slaves.

CHRISTINE.   Have you had affairs before?

LARRY.   Never! That kiss was the first kiss I ever had out of the house.

CHRISTINE.   I wish you hadn't told me that.

LARRY. Well, I did.

CHRISTINE. It puts a lot more responsibility on the situation.

LARRY. Good! Why shouldn't you feel responsible? The fact of the matter is as soon as you realize that I am not a dream, that I'm really here, and who I really am, at that moment you will head for the door!

CHRISTINE. I don't know about that.

LARRY. I do.

CHRISTINE. Do you think you know who I really am?

LARRY. No. But if I did ...

CHRISTINE. But if you did...?

LARRY. Ah, shit. *(He looks at her and kisses her.)* That was a wonderful, wonderful ... kiss. Goddamnit.

CHRISTINE. Why do I like you?

LARRY. I don't know. Do you really like me?

CHRISTINE. Yes.

LARRY. You really do?

CHRISTINE. Yes.

LARRY. That makes me very happy.

CHRISTINE. Good.

LARRY. This is the strangest conversation I've ever had.

CHRISTINE. This is the strangest conversation I've ever had.

LARRY. Do you think it's because we went to that lecture?

CHRISTINE. Are you trying to hatch an alibi for your wife?

LARRY. But why couldn't I remember your name, Christine?!

CHRISTINE. Why can you remember it now?

LARRY. You're a receptionist?

CHRISTINE. A very busy receptionist. Headset and a microphone. I just hear voices and respond in this very automatic way all day long.

LARRY. And you like that?

CHRISTINE. It's great. I don't exist. I'm a piece of wire. It takes all my time and all my attention and it means absolutely nothing.

LARRY. I don't understand you. I know you're saying something that's at the core of something, but what is it?!

CHRISTINE. What's so great about being you, Larry?

LARRY.   Nothing.

CHRISTINE.   Exactly. Exactly.

LARRY.   You said there's still something wrong with you.

CHRISTINE.   Yes.

LARRY.   I think I know what it is.

CHRISTINE.   What?

LARRY.   You've had some kind of experience and nobody can know what it is because it has nothing to do with words so you can't share it, and that makes you lonely.

CHRISTINE.   No, that's not it.

LARRY.   That was a little close, wasn't it?

CHRISTINE.   What do you mean?

LARRY.   What kind of dancer were you?

CHRISTINE.   Modern. Abstract. We used video.

LARRY.   Do you still see the other dancers?

CHRISTINE.   No. The language of dancers is dance. I couldn't talk to them anymore.

LARRY.   Do you miss them?

CHRISTINE.   No.

LARRY.   Do you miss dancing?

CHRISTINE.   Yes. Yes. *(He takes her hand. She is sad.)*

LARRY.   Look at all these fingers.

CHRISTINE.   Do you love your wife?

LARRY.   Of course.

CHRISTINE.   In proofreading, one proofreader reads against the other. They watch out for each other. Their object is to agree. But each of them must listen very carefully to the other. The agreement must be real.

LARRY.   I don't really care, at this moment, how my story turns out. I'm deeply, deeply bored with my own story. But I like being alive. I like being here with you.

CHRISTINE.   Is your wife's name really Babette?!

LARRY.   Yes. *(They laugh.)* I'm not laughing at her expense.

CHRISTINE.   I know.

LARRY.   There are so many jokes in my life. If I say my life out loud, I see it's full of jokes. But you know the whole story of my life, if I said the whole story of my life out loud, all the events, I don't think it has anything to do with who I am.

CHRISTINE.   Oh, I bet it does.

LARRY.   No, no. It doesn't. *Your* life, yes. The events of your life strike me as having something to do with your true story. You fell in a hole. It's so graphic! But me selling bonds, selling health, mortgaging the apartment, the twins ...

CHRISTINE.   Babette.

LARRY.   Babette, Umbria, my medical problems ...

CHRISTINE.   What medical problems?

LARRY.   Oh, I didn't mention that? I have a lazy eye. I HAD a lazy eye, a wandering eye. Six operations later it doesn't wander anymore and who gives a shit?

CHRISTINE.   You mean it didn't look at you?

LARRY.   Exactly! It didn't look at you. NOW it looks at you! The pain, the money that went into that.... Well, it was worth it. I felt bad about it. Vanity.

CHRISTINE.   I can understand that.

LARRY.   I wanted to look attractive.

CHRISTINE.   You are attractive.

LARRY.   No. I am?

CHRISTINE.   Whatever that means. Yes.

LARRY.   You think so?

CHRISTINE.   I wouldn't have kissed you.

LARRY.   If I had a wandering eye.

CHRISTINE.   You do have a wandering eye.

LARRY.   True! Before it was on the outside, now it's my character! Now I truly do have a wandering eye and you'd never know it to look at me. Six operations later.

CHRISTINE.   They pushed it in.

LARRY.   That's right. They shoved the wandering eye in. My third eye. The one that drifts. Like one of those space telescopes. Now it's at my core. *(He struggles with an emotion.)*

CHRISTINE.   Hey. That's right.

LARRY.   I'm sorry. Jeez. Emotion.

CHRISTINE.   No, it's good.

LARRY.   I'm okay now.

CHRISTINE.   Why bother to be?

LARRY.   I just sometimes feel this thing rise. It's like Hawaii being born. Except it doesn't get born. It sinks again. Some

Supreme Court keeps it down. The weight of some authority. I have all this feeling, but the days are small. They're too small. It's like I'm melting copper and tin. But I have so much more bronze than I need to fill the form, lose the wax, make the life. But I hate to just spill it!

CHRISTINE. Come here.

LARRY. I'm useless.

CHRISTINE. I doubt that.

LARRY. Don't.

CHRISTINE. What upset you?

LARRY. I was upset. It's when I feel a little good that I know how bad I feel. You provided a little ... easement, so now I feel really lousy.

CHRISTINE. Think about nothing.

LARRY. I can't think about nothing. That's not a skill of mine. I guess I can't be in the club. Can you do that?

CHRISTINE. Me? I'm the Queen of Nothing.

LARRY. Is that by blood or marriage?

CHRISTINE. Accident of nature.

LARRY. You mean the accident? That accident you had.

CHRISTINE. Yeah. At first I didn't know that I was, but I was. And then, after a time, I knew I was a being in a bed. For a long time that's all I knew. I could hear my breathing, which to me seemed like the universe through which I passed. My body, which had been everything to me, was gone. No memories, not for a long time. Then just pictures without language. Then my body came back. And pain. Struggle. Other people. Language. Life is very hard. Very, very hard. You shouldn't feel bad you suffer. Why wouldn't you? It breaks your heart. The facts of life. The tyranny of the body. These outward appearances. What we do for show. All these temporary situations and arrangements we have to believe are permanent. The emotion underneath everything is so strong.

LARRY. I don't know what you mean.

CHRISTINE. Yes, you do. The only think you don't understand is the power of surrender and the freedom of nothing. I felt it when I came back. I saw how hard it is. It made me feel for people. It made me feel for myself. I used to think if

55

I could pull the bread out of someone else's mouth I wouldn't starve, and I lived my life like that. Mean. I had some things then, some things I don't have now. I could dance.... But I wouldn't go back, I wouldn't want to go back. It was an illusion anyway. A bunch of empty coconuts. We're turning in the dark, in the depths of the ocean. Luminous creatures looking for food in a world of spirit. When my mother looked at me and said: Christine, you've changed. You've changed, Christine. It made me shiver. And a voice in me said, It's true, I'm not the woman I was! Like that old man when he looked at you and saw you and he stopped your selling. What was it he said? What are you doing here?

LARRY.   Me?

CHRISTINE.   What are you doing here, Larry?

LARRY.   You seem like a nice woman. I thought it might be nice ...

CHRISTINE.   No.

LARRY.   Yes. Alright. Ah, I might as well be dead.

CHRISTINE.   I don't think so.

LARRY.   But you don't necessarily know anything about it. Speaking to me from beyond the grave or wherever the hell you are. Maybe I am dead and this is just — the period before I actively begin to rot.

CHRISTINE.   No. You're doing things.

LARRY.   That old man didn't change me!

CHRISTINE.   I'm not saying he did. But maybe he gave you a shove.

LARRY.   Alright! Maybe things are a little better! I mean as a result of that encounter with the maker of cakes my outer landscape isn't as completely unlike my inner landscape as it was when I was a seller of bonds. Or at the health club answering questions about pool rules. But my apparent biography is still a crock of hypocrisy and shit!

CHRISTINE.   I don't think things are as bad as you think they are.

LARRY.   They're pretty bad. Now I'm out on dates, I'm going to crackpot lectures. Did I tell you I tried to take up painting?

CHRISTINE. No.

LARRY. Well, I can't paint! That much I know.

CHRISTINE. What did you paint?

LARRY. Doors! I just painted doors! But the doors never opened. And the doors were.... Well, I can't paint! And I can't be married! And I hate being single! And though I have had some tender feelings in my life, made some money, known some success, had some pleasure, maybe been a good father once or twice ...

CHRISTINE. Do you feel like you just haven't lived?

LARRY. No, I've lived. I've lived. But it's a train wreck. It's a pointless jig. I have danced a pointless jig. And under that, almost like a mockery, I see this, feel this vast pattern, this gargantuan book of meaning. Like the plates that slide under the crust of the earth, like the pattern in the swirl of the Milky Way. It's there! That's clear to me! But it's there and I'm here and never the twain shall meet!

CHRISTINE. That's funny.

LARRY. Is it?

CHRISTINE. Yeah.

LARRY. That's irritating. Why?

CHRISTINE. Because all these things you see out there, I see in here. But I don't see them out there like you do.

LARRY. You don't?

CHRISTINE. No. Out there, well, that's where I see the train wreck. I think, Give up on out there. It's senseless. Whatever order there is, whatever meaning, whatever goodness, evil, strength, beauty, whatever makes sense comes from the inside.

LARRY. HOW CAN YOU SAY THAT!

CHRISTINE. Do you remember my name?

LARRY. CHRISTINE.

CHRISTINE. Very good.

LARRY. Meaningful Chance. That was the fat woman's subject. And beyond that, if you recall, Divination. Reading into what's right here. The cards, the bones, the dice. Seeing the Future folded into the Present. I know that if I had the skill, I could read the Future in the stars tonight.

CHRISTINE. And I know that if I had the ability, I could

see the Future in you.

LARRY.   Do you really feel when you look at me that I make sense?

CHRISTINE.   Yes.

LARRY.   Like the Milky Way makes sense?

CHRISTINE.   Well, I wouldn't know about that. To me the Milky Way is fabulous gibberish.

LARRY.   Amazing. And I thought you were smart.

CHRISTINE.   Oh, so now you know something?

LARRY.   Some few things are obvious to me. Like perhaps it would be for the best if I were blotted off the face of the earth. And that the earth is good.

CHRISTINE.   You are good. And I'll tell you, that's a dangerous line of thinking.

LARRY.   Why's that?

CHRISTINE.   When people get it into their heads that the earth is good and they are shit, the next thing you know they become a certain kind of fanatic.

LARRY.   What kind of fanatic?

CHRISTINE.   A save the planet, kill the people kind of fanatic. The only thing wrong with the environment is that I'm in it kind of thinking.

LARRY.   Well, I'm not that deep into the idea.

CHRISTINE.   You can't hate yourself and love.

LARRY.   I see what you're saying.

CHRISTINE.   You can't even dislike yourself and love.

LARRY.   Huh. Then I have never loved and I never shall love. But I have loved.

CHRISTINE.   You have?

LARRY.   I did like myself then though.

CHRISTINE.   So why don't you now?

LARRY.   When I liked myself I didn't know myself very well. Now that I've gotten to know the man, I don't care for him.

CHRISTINE.   Then you can't love.

LARRY.   Can you?

CHRISTINE.   No. *(They kiss.)*

LARRY.   I feel something.

CHRISTINE.   Me too. *(They kiss again.)* What do you feel?

LARRY.   I'm not dead. Life. I feel life I guess. What do you feel?
CHRISTINE.   Envy. Envy of you. *(She is on the verge of breaking. She reaches for him, as one would reach out to touch a ghost. He understands for the first time what she has lost.)*
LARRY.   You're gonna be okay.
CHRISTINE.   I was a dancer.

THE END

PROPERTY LIST

Chopsticks (LARRY, CHRISTINE)
Plates of Thai food (LARRY, CHRISTINE)
Beers (LARRY, CHRISTINE)
Soup (LARRY, CHRISTINE)
Glasses of water (LARRY, CHRISTINE, SERVER)
Tray of beverages (SERVER)
Candle (SERVER)
Photograph (SERVER)
Hot tea (SERVER)
Check for meal (SERVER)

NEW PLAYS

- **SMASH by Jeffrey Hatcher.** Based on the novel, AN UNSOCIAL SOCIALIST by George Bernard Shaw, the story centers on a millionaire Socialist who leaves his bride on their wedding day because he fears his passion for her will get in the way of his plans to overthrow the British government. *"SMASH is witty, cunning, intelligent, and skillful."* *–Seattle Weekly.* *"SMASH is a wonderfully high-style British comedy of manners that evokes the world of Shaw's high-minded heroes and heroines, but shaped by a post modern sensibility."* *–Seattle Herald.* [5M, 5W] ISBN: 0-8222-1553-5

- **PRIVATE EYES by Steven Dietz.** A comedy of suspicion in which nothing is ever quite what it seems. *"Steven Dietz's ... Pirandellian smooch to the mercurial nature of theatrical illusion and romantic truth, Dietz's spiraling structure and breathless pacing provide enough of an oxygen rush to revive any moribund audience member ... Dietz's mastery of playmaking ... is cause for kudos."* *–The Village Voice.* *"The cleverest and most artful piece presented at the 21st annual [Humana] festival was PRIVATE EYES by writer-director Steven Dietz."* *–The Chicago Tribune.* [3M, 2W] ISBN: 0-8222-1619-1

- **DIMLY PERCEIVED THREATS TO THE SYSTEM by Jon Klein.** Reality and fantasy overlap with hilarious results as this unforgettable family attempts to survive the nineties. *"Here's a play whose point about fractured families goes to the heart, mind -- and ears."* *–The Washington Post.* *" ... an end-of-the millennium comedy about a family on the verge of a nervous breakdown ... Trenchant and hilarious ... "* *–The Baltimore Sun.* [2M, 4W] ISBN: 0-8222-1677-9

- **HONOUR by Joanna Murray-Smith.** In a series of intense confrontations, a wife, husband, lover and daughter negotiate the forces of passion, lust, history, responsibility and honour. *"Tight, crackling dialogue (usually played out in punchy verbal duels) captures characters unable to deal with emotions ... Murray-Smith effectively places her characters in situations that strip away pretense."* *–Variety.* *"HONOUR might just capture a few honors of its own."* *–Time Out Magazine.* [1M, 3W] ISBN: 0-8222-1683-3

- **NINE ARMENIANS by Leslie Ayvazian.** A revealing portrait of three generations of an Armenian-American family. *" ... Ayvazian's obvious personal exploration ... is evocative, and her picture of an American Life colored nostalgically by an increasingly alien ethnic tradition, is persuasively embedded into a script of a certain supple grace ... "* *–The NY Post.* *"... NINE ARMENIANS is a warm, likable work that benefits from ... Ayvazian's clear-headed insight into the dynamics of a close-knit family ... "* *–Variety.* [5M, 5W] ISBN: 0-8222-1602-7

- **PSYCHOPATHIA SEXUALIS by John Patrick Shanley.** Fetishes and psychiatry abound in this scathing comedy about a man and his father's argyle socks. *"John Patrick Shanley's new play, PSYCHOPATHIA SEXUALIS is ... perfectly poised between daffy comedy and believable human neurosis which Shanley combines so well ... "* *–The LA Times.* *"John Patrick Shanley's PSYCHOPATHIA SEXUALIS is a salty boulevard comedy with a bittersweet theme ... "* *–New York Magazine.* *"A tour de force of witty, barbed dialogue."* *–Variety.* [3M, 2W] ISBN: 0-8222-1615-9

DRAMATISTS PLAY SERVICE, INC.
440 Park Avenue South, New York, NY 10016 212-683-8960 Fax 212-213-1539
postmaster@dramatists.com www.dramatists.com

NEW PLAYS

• **A QUESTION OF MERCY by David Rabe.** The Obie Award-winning playwright probes the sensitive and controversial issue of doctor-assisted suicide in the age of AIDS in this poignant drama. *"There are many devastating ironies in Mr. Rabe's beautifully considered, piercingly clear-eyed work ... " –The NY Times.* "With unsettling candor and disturbing insight, the play arouses pity and understanding of a troubling subject ... Rabe's provocative tale is an affirmation of dignity that rings clear and true." –Variety.* [6M, 1W] ISBN: 0-8222-1643-4

• **A DOLL'S HOUSE by Henrik Ibsen, adapted by Frank McGuinness. Winner of the 1997 Tony Award for best revival.** *"New, raw, gut-twisting and gripping. Easily the hottest drama this season." –USA Today.* "Bold, brilliant and alive." –The Wall Street Journal.* "A thunderclap of an evening that takes your breath away." –Time.* "The stuff of Broadway legend." –Associated Press.* [4M, 4W, 2 boys] ISBN: 0-8222-1636-1

• **THE WAITING ROOM by Lisa Loomer.** Three women from different centuries meet in a doctor's waiting room in this dark comedy about the timeless quest for beauty -- and its cost. *" ... THE WAITING ROOM ... is a bold, risky melange of conflicting elements that is ... terrifically moving ... There's no resisting the fierce emotional pull of the play." –The NY Times.* " ... one of the high points of this year's Off-Broadway season ... THE WAITING ROOM is well worth a visit." –Back Stage.* [7M, 4W, flexible casting] ISBN: 0-8222-1594-2

• **MR. PETERS' CONNECTIONS by Arthur Miller.** Mr. Miller describes the protagonist as existing in a dream-like state when the mind is "freed to roam from real memories to conjectures, from trivialities to tragic insights, from terror of death to glorying in one's being alive." With this memory play, the Tony Award and Pulitzer Prize-winner reaffirms his stature as the world's foremost dramatist. *" ... a cross between Joycean stream-of-consciousness and Strindberg's dream plays, sweetened with a dose of William Saroyan's philosophical whimsy ... CONNECTIONS is most intriguing ... Miller scholars will surely find many connections of their own to make between this work and the author's earlier plays." –The NY Times.* [5M, 3W] ISBN: 0-8222-1687-6

• **THE STEWARD OF CHRISTENDOM by Sebastian Barry.** A freely imagined portrait of the author's great-grandfather, the last Chief Superintendent of the Dublin Metropolitan Police. *"MAGNIFICENT ... the cool, elegiac eye of James Joyce's THE DEAD; the bleak absurdity of Samuel Beckett's lost, primal characters; the cosmic anger of KING LEAR ..." –The NY Times.* "Sebastian Barry's compassionate imaging of an ancestor he never knew is among the most poignant onstage displays of humanity in recent memory." –Variety.* [5M, 4W] ISBN: 0-8222-1609-4

• **SYMPATHETIC MAGIC by Lanford Wilson. Winner of the 1997 Obie for best play.** The mysteries of the universe, and of human and artistic creation, are explored in this award-winning play. *"Lanford Wilson's idiosyncratic SYMPATHETIC MAGIC is his BEST PLAY YET ... the rare play you WANT ... chock-full of ideas, incidents, witty or poetic lines, scientific and philosophical argument ... you'll find your intellectual faculties racing." –New York Magazine.* "The script is like a fully notated score, next to which most new plays are cursory lead sheets." –The Village Voice.* [5M, 3W] ISBN: 0-8222-1630-2

DRAMATISTS PLAY SERVICE, INC.
440 Park Avenue South, New York, NY 10016 212-683-8960 Fax 212-213-1539
postmaster@dramatists.com www.dramatists.com